DK READERS

Level 4

Days of the Knights
Volcanoes and Other Natural
  Disasters
Pirates: Raiders of the High
  Seas
Horse Heroes
Trojan Horse
Micro Monsters
Going for Gold!
Extreme Machines
Flying Ace: The Story of
  Amelia Earhart
Robin Hood
Black Beauty
Free at Last! The Story of
  Martin Luther King, Jr.
Joan of Arc
Spooky Spinechillers
Welcome to The Globe! The
  Story of Shakespeare's
  Theater
Antarctic Adventure
Space Station
Atlantis: The Lost City?
Dinosaur Detectives
Danger on the Mountain:
  Scaling the World's Highest
  Peaks
Crime Busters
The Story of Muhammad Ali
First Flight: The Story of the
  Wright Brothers
LEGO: Race for Survival

NFL: NFL's Greatest Upsets
NFL: Rumbling Running
  Backs
WCW: Going for Goldberg
WCW: Feel the Sting
MLB: Strikeout Kings
MLB: Super Shortstops: Jeter,
  Nomar, and A-Rod
MLB: The Story of the New
  York Yankees
JLA: Batman's Guide to Crime
  and Detection
JLA: Superman's Guide to the
  Universe
The Story of the X-Men: How
  it all Began
Creating the X-Men: How
  Comic Books Come to Life
Spider-Man's Amazing Powers
The Story of Spider-Man
The Incredible Hulk's Book of
  Strength
The Story of the Incredible
  Hulk
Transformers Armada: The
  Awakening
Transformers Armada: The
  Quest

A Note to Parents

DK READERS is a compelling program for beginning readers, designed in conjunction with leading literacy experts.

Beautiful illustrations and superb full-color photographs combine with engaging, easy-to-read stories to offer a fresh approach to each subject in the series. Each DK READER is guaranteed to capture a child's interest while developing his or her reading skills, general knowledge, and love of reading.

The four levels of DK READERS are aimed at different reading abilities, enabling you to choose the books that are exactly right for your child:

Level 1 – Beginning to read
Level 2 – Beginning to read alone
Level 3 – Reading alone
Level 4 – Proficient readers

The "normal" age at which a child begins to read can be anywhere from three to eight years old, so these levels are only a general guideline.

No matter which level you select, you can be sure that you are helping your child learn to read, then read to learn!

LONDON, NEW YORK, MELBOURNE,
MUNICH, AND DELHI

Editor Kate Phelps
Designer Sooz Bellerby
Series Editor Alastair Dougall
Production Jenny Jacoby
Picture Researcher Julia Harris-Voss

First American Edition, 2003
04 05 06 07 10 9 8 7 6 5 4 3 2
Published in the United States by DK Publishing, Inc.
375 Hudson Street, New York, New York 10014

Library of Congress Cataloging-in-Publication Data

Donkin, Andrew.
  Transformers Armada : the quest / by Andrew Donkin.-- 1st American
ed.
    p. cm. -- (DK readers)
  Summary: Relates the history of the Autobots, Decepticons, and
Mini-Cons, and the story of their battle for control of the universe.
  ISBN 0-7894-9804-9 (hardcover) -- ISBN 0-7894-9742-5 (pbk.)
  [1. Science fiction.] I. Title. II. Series: Dorling Kindersley
readers.
  PZ7.D7175Tr 2003
  [Fic]--dc21
                                2003003904

Color reproduction by Colourscan, Singapore
Printed and bound in China by L Rex Printing Co., Ltd.

The publisher thanks the following for their kind permission
to reproduce their photographs:
c=center; t=top; b=bottom; l=left; r=right

Bryan And Cherry Alexander Photography:
21tr. **Corbis:** Archivio Iconografico, S.A. 26cl; Horace Bristol 21cr;
Hubert Stadler 33tr; Latreille François/CDP/Sygma 20tl. **Mary Evans
Picture Library:** 42tl. **The Picture Desk:** British Museum/ Eileen Tweedy
32cl. **Science Photo Library:** 14bl, 24bl; Bernard Edmater 30tl; British
Antarctic Survey 16bl; Jeremy Bishop 36tl; Mark Garlick 27tr; National
Institutes of Health 40cl; Philippe Plailly 25tr; Simon Fraser 16tl.

All other photographs © Dorling Kindersley.
For further information see: www.dkimages.com

Discover more at
www.dk.com

Contents

Alien robots	4
Power struggle	6
The Autobots	8
The Decepticons	9
The Mini-Cons	10
The kids	12
The quest	14
The lost city	22
Volcano adventure	30
Star Saber	38
Glossary	48

DK READERS
PROFICIENT READERS 4

The Quest

Written by Andrew Donkin

Giant size
In robot mode,
Transformers
look like 30-foot
(10-meter) tall
humanoid
robots.

**Power to
change**
Transformers
can change into
many forms,
including
weapons,
machines, cars,
tanks, and
fighter aircraft.

Alien robots

Transformers are a race of living,
thinking alien robots. These mighty
machines are as tall as a four-story
building and possess great strength
and extraordinary powers.

All Transformers are capable of
altering their structure. By sheer
willpower, they can convert their
robot bodies into other forms of
mechanical equipment.

Transforming from "robot
mode" into "vehicle mode,"
they change from
humanoid robot
into a machine such
as a car, a tank, or
even a jet. Of all
the races in the
known cosmos,
their abilities are
truly unique.

The Transformers' home
planet is Cybertron, a glittering

world of silver machinery. For centuries, the Transformers lived in harmony, but then an evil faction of the robots arose. They were hellbent on taking over the planet, and the peace was shattered forever.

Transformers' technology and weaponry is thousands of years more advanced than Earth science.

Capital city
Iacon is a teeming metropolis of art, science, learning, and culture.

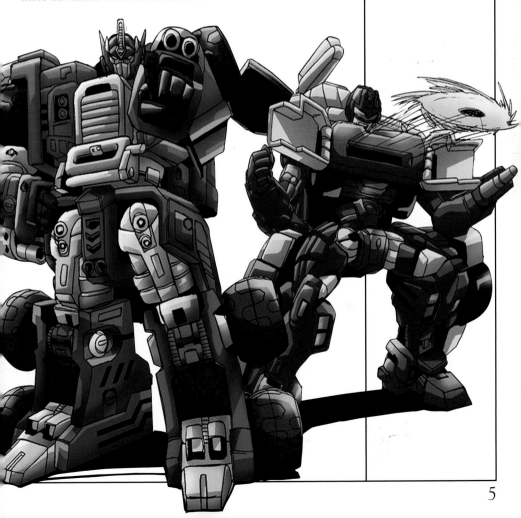

Vehicle mode
Autobot leader,
Optimus Prime,
can transform
into a powerful
truck complete
with trailer.

Power struggle

The evil race of
Transformers known as Decepticons
were determined to rule Cybertron
and the whole Universe.

The only thing standing in the
Decepticons' way were the Autobots,
a race of robots who believed in
peace. The Autobots realized that
the only way to stop the Decepticons
was to face them in hand-to-hand
combat. Each faction tried to use its
amazing transforming powers to
overcome the enemy, but the two
opposing groups were evenly
matched. The many battles that
followed became known
as the Cybertronian
wars. These civil wars
have lasted for almost nine
million years and have

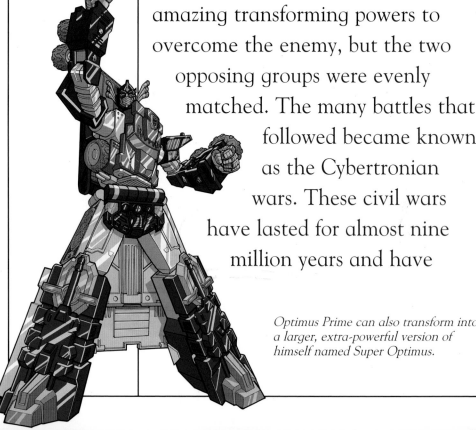

*Optimus Prime can also transform into
a larger, extra-powerful version of
himself named Super Optimus.*

spanned many generations of Transformers. The leader of the Decepticons is the vile Megatron. The Autobots are led by one of the most powerful Transformers of all time, Optimus Prime.

The two factions are locked in a deadly dispute. Will the dark forces win or can Optimus and his men save the Universe?

The planet Cybertron has been the scene of the Transformers' civil war for many centuries.

Fire power
Megatron's main weapon is his tank cannon, which can lay waste to an entire battlefield.

Tank attack
The evil Megatron can transform himself into a supertank equipped with deadly grabber claws.

Hot Shot
When Hot Shot transforms into vehicle mode, he becomes a superspeedy sports car.

Red Alert
Optimus Prime's right-hand man, Red Alert, is also an experienced medic and has saved many lives on the battlefield. He transforms into an emergency rescue vehicle.

The Autobots

The leader of the Autobots is Optimus Prime. Optimus will always try to find a peaceful solution to any problem. When that's not possible, though, he is a fierce and brave warrior. The Autobot leader believes that all living creatures have a right to freedom.

Optimus Prime is backed up by his three Autobot teammates: the headstrong Hot Shot; repair expert Red Alert; and Optimus Prime's old friend Smokescreen.

Smokescreen's crane arm is immensely powerful.

The Decepticons

Megatron is the leader of the evil Decepticons. His one goal is to take control of Cybertron and use it as a base to conquer the rest of the Universe. He is an experienced warrior and is utterly selfish.

Megatron has three main Decepticon minions: the battle-hardened veteran Demolishor, who is loyal only to Megatron; the young and power-hungry Starscream; and the trigger-happy Cyclonus, who is always trying to impress Megatron.

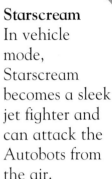

Starscream
In vehicle mode, Starscream becomes a sleek jet fighter and can attack the Autobots from the air.

Cyclonus
This reckless young Decepticon transforms into an army helicopter.

Mini-Cons

Mini-Cons
Mini-Cons are humanoid robots, about the same height as a person. They have large eyes and friendly faces.

Transportation
Like the bigger races of Transformers, Mini-Cons can also change into vehicles.

The planet of Cybertron was also home to a *third* race of Transformers. They were peace-loving robots called Mini-Cons.

Although small in size and meek in manner, the Mini-Cons held the balance of power between the Decepticons and the Autobots.

The Mini-Cons were worker robots until one day it was discovered that when a Mini-Con joined, or powerlinked, with a larger Transformer, it increased

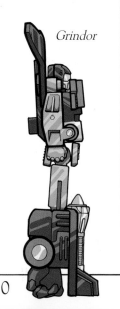

Grindor

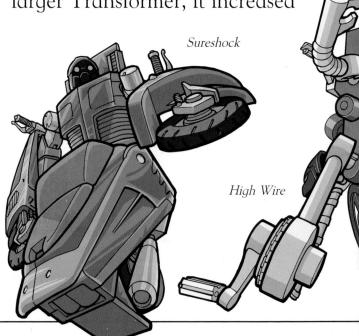

Sureshock

High Wire

the big Transformer's
power to incredible levels.

The Decepticons set about
capturing as many Mini-Cons as
possible to enslave them for their
war effort. The Autobots were
forced to use the Mini-Cons, too,
just to avoid defeat.

The powerboost the Mini-Cons
gave the Transformers meant that
the battles between the Autobots
and Decepticons became ever
more ferocious and
devastating. So it was
decided that in order to save
their planet from destruction,
the Mini-Cons should leave
Cybertron forever.

**Strength in
numbers**
Grindor,
Sureshock, and
High Wire can
combine
together to
form a super
Mini-Con
called
Perceptor.

The kids

Ancient Cybertron legends tell how the Mini-Cons left the Transformers' home planet with their entire race aboard one spaceship. A skeleton crew manned the ship while the rest of the Mini-Cons went into a state of hibernation.

The ship was damaged while passing through numerous warp gates and drifted through space until eventually it collided with Earth's Moon. The collision was disastrous. The ship broke in two, scattering sleeping Mini-Cons all over Earth and the Moon. The Mini-Cons lay hidden, asleep for millions of years until someone woke them up…

Exploring a mountain cave, school friends, Rad Carlos, and Alexis found one of the Mini-Cons.

Rad
Rad is the 14 year old who discovers the Mini-Cons on Earth and sets off the new Transformers war! High Wire is his Mini-Con partner.

Carlos
Carlos is Rad's best friend and is an expert on a skateboard. His Mini-Con partner is called Grindor.

Its awakening sent a signal back to Cybertron and alerted the Transfomers to the lost Mini-Cons' location. The Decepticons arrived on Earth, looking for the Mini-Cons. The Autobots quickly followed, determined to stop them. Befriending the Autobots on their arrival, the kids are now vital members of the team.

Thanks to the Mini-Cons, the Transformers' galactic war has spread to a new battleground… a small blue planet called Earth!

Alexis
Thirteen-year-old Alexis is partnered with the Mini-Con Sureshock, who transforms into a scooter for her to ride.

Rad discovers a glowing green object in the cave, little knowing he is waking up a Mini-Con and starting a galactic war!

Antarctica

Antarctica
The landmass at the South Pole is called Antarctica. This frozen wasteland has an area of over 5 million sq. miles (13 million sq. kilometers).

Polar first
The first person to reach the South Pole was Norwegian explorer Roald Amundsen, in 1911.

The quest

Rad and his friends, Alexis and Carlos, had become mixed up in the Transformers' war on Earth. Here is the story of one of their exciting adventures.

The evil Decepticons had been trying to grab as many Mini-Cons as they could so they could use their power to take over the Universe. It was up to the Autobots, along with Carlos, Alexis, and Rad, to stop them by finding the Mini-Cons first!

The kids had been in the Autobots' base all morning. Hot Shot had been getting on everyone's nerves by complaining that Red Alert was more of a mechanic than a warrior. Optimus Prime tried to set him right on that one, but Hot Shot still wasn't convinced.

When the alarm sounded, the kids knew that a new Mini-Con signal had come in and that

everyone had to move fast.
One amazing warp-gate
journey later and they found
themselves in the snowy
wastes of Antarctica!

Blinding white sheets of ice and
snow spread out in all directions.
A Mini-Con was hidden somewhere,
and the Autobots had to find it
before Megatron and his cronies did.

Ice sheet
The average
thickness of
the ice sheet
that covers
Antarctica is
5,900 feet
(1,800 meters).

But the Transformers' vehicles weren't designed for such harsh conditions and freezing temperatures and had come to a grinding halt. Red Alert made some emergency repairs just so the robots could keep moving. He fitted all the Autobots with special snow traction tires so they could grip the ice. Then Jolt, the helicopter Mini-Con, powerlinked with Hot Shot. Together they could speed across the slippery snowfield. Carlos eagerly climbed inside Hot Shot ready for some action.

"Keep your eyes open," said Carlos excitedly as they set off. "That Mini-Con could be anywhere around here."

As they hurtled across the ice sheet in the direction of the Mini-Con's signal, a dark shape appeared in the sky

above them. It was the Decepticon
Starscream in jet fighter mode.
Disaster! He swooped toward them in
a low arc, firing wildly with both
guns! Trying to escape, Hot Shot
with Carlos inside drove at full speed
straight over a huge cliff!

Bottom heavy
Sometimes ice breaks free and floats out to sea as an iceberg. When you see an iceberg, you are only seeing part of it. Eighty percent of its bulk is always hidden under the water!

Carlos screamed as they plummeted down the deep chasm. Jolt, still attached to the rear of Hot Shot, started his rotor blades on full power. He saved the day. With a little help from Jolt, pretty soon Hot Shot was driving straight up the sheer face of the chasm wall. As they raced up, Carlos caught sight of a bright green light embedded in the rockface.

"Look, there's the Mini-Con! We've found it!" said Carlos, but there was no time to stop.

As they made it out of the chasm, Hot Shot was in for a nasty surprise.

Jolt saves Hot Shot and Carlos by starting his rotor blades. They are soon climbing up the chasm wall.

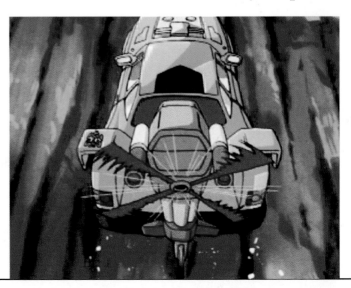

The Decepticons were waiting, and he was outnumbered four to one.

"Excellent. Let's get him!" said Megatron menacingly.

Hot Shot took action. He drove straight at Starscream, sending him crashing to the ground.

Carlos dived out of Hot Shot's sports car so the Autobot could transform back into robot mode. That was a big mistake. Within a few seconds, the unlucky Hot Shot was pinned down by the deadly firepower of all the Decepticons!

Anti-freeze
Fish who live in the polar regions, such as the Antarctic cod, have special chemicals in their bodies to stop their blood from freezing.

On his own, Hot Shot is no match for Megatron and his evil Decepticon soldiers.

Eternal day
In the summer at the poles, there is bright daylight for weeks on end. In the winter, there is pitch black night for more than one month.

Cyclonus leaped forward so he could fire at Hot Shot from point blank range. Just as he was going to pull the trigger, something grabbed his shoulder and jerked him violently backward.

It was Red Alert. He'd saved Hot Shot's life. Without thinking of his own safety, Red Alert leaped into battle, drawing the Decepticons' fire away from Hot Shot. After that moment, Hot Shot never doubted that Red Alert was a real warrior ever again.

Red Alert risks his own life to save Hot Shot.

When Optimus Prime came sliding down a snowdrift to join the battle, the three Decepticons knew they were defeated, and the cowards warped out.

Down in the canyon, Starscream was punching the Mini-Con loose from the rockface. Carlos and Rad tried to stop him, but it was too late. He'd gotten it! They needn't have worried. Jolt, in helicopter mode, swooped down and snatched it right out of his hand!

Starscream grabs the Mini-Con from from out of the icy rockface.

World's least inhabited place
Antarctica is huge, but it is populated by just a few hundred people, most of them scientists in research bases.

The Arctic
Unlike Antarctica, the ice at the Arctic, or North Pole, has no solid land underneath it. Since it is cold all year round, the ocean has frozen, forming thick ice.

Special vessels explore deep under the ocean. The bathysphere *Trieste* reached a record-breaking depth of 35,800 feet (10,912 meters) in 1960.

bathysphere

Creature of the deep
In the black depths of the ocean, the angler fish has a light on its head to attract smaller fish, which it then gulps down.

The lost city

When the kids and their robot friends came out of the warp gate this time, they found themselves deep under the Atlantic Ocean. Carlos, Alexis, and Rad were safely tucked up in the cabin of Optimus Prime.

All the Autobots had transformed into vehicle mode. Red Alert had made a few adjustments so they could travel under the water.

The Autobots were homing in on a Mini-Con signal that seemed to be coming from deep under the sea.

"Scans say we're really close, guys," said Alexis.

"You're not going to believe this!" exclaimed Hot Shot, coming to a sudden halt.

Ahead of them the headlights of the vehicles illuminated a huge temple wall. It looked like the ancient ruins of a lost civilization, like Atlantis.

"There's a whole city down here!" said Carlos.

Before they could explore any further, energy blasts exploded all around them!

"It's an ambush!" said Hot Shot.

Gulper eel
This bizarre creature lives deep in the ocean. It is little more than a huge mouth and a baglike stomach.

Ancient city
The legendary civilization of Atlantis was said to have been destroyed by a flood.

Optimus Prime in truck mode drives the kids up the steps and into the mysterious ancient underwater city.

City tales
The Greek thinker Plato is famous for recording the legend of Atlantis. But was it a true story or did he make it up?

Megatron and his dastardly Decepticons had also traced the new Mini-Con signal. They'd gotten there first and were lying in wait to ambush the good guys.

Hot Shot transformed back into robot mode and fired a distress flair, but he wasn't calling for help. The bright light dazzled the Decepticons, and the Autobots and their young friends made their escape.

There was still trouble ahead, though. The Decepticons' blasts had shattered the windshield of Optimus Prime's truck, and the cabin was filling with seawater. Hot Shot quickly ripped open the doors of the ancient city's largest building and Optimus Prime drove inside.

"Hang on kids, I see an air pocket!" said Optimus.

They reached it just in time.

Optimus sent the kids to find the new Mini-Con while he went back to deal with Megatron. As they entered the central square of the temple, the kids set off a hologram of a young girl.

"Welcome," she said, "I've been expecting you."

3D images
Holograms are 3D photos made by lasers. The bottom half of this glass is real; the top half is a hologram.

The girl told of the terrible wars that led to the destruction of her ancient city.

Atlantean priestess
Some people think that a mysterious stone statue called the Lady of Elche found in Spain might really show a priestess from Atlantis.

The hologram girl told the story of what had happened to her city.

"Thousands of years ago my people found what you call Mini-Cons. Three of them combined to become a powerful weapon called the Star Saber. We used it to power our city, and for a while we flourished. Before long, however, we used it to wage war on others. Our people could not control its power, and in the process we destroyed ourselves!"

The temple floor suddenly shook.

"What on earth is going on out there?" said Alexis.

The kids guessed there was a pretty fierce battle being fought outside between their friends and the evil Decepticons.

"We have to find that Mini-Con and fast!" Rad said.

The hologram's warning had really affected Carlos. He was starting to think that maybe everyone would be better off *without* the Mini-Con.

Just then a huge fist smashed through the temple wall.

Underwater search
Divers have been looking for the ruins of Atlantis for a long time.

God of the sea
Poseidon was the Greek god of the sea and oceans.

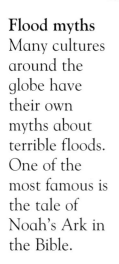

Flood myths
Many cultures around the globe have their own myths about terrible floods. One of the most famous is the tale of Noah's Ark in the Bible.

Megatron had broken through the Autobots' defense and was only looking for one thing.

"Where's that Mini-Con?" he snarled angrily.

He ordered his own Mini-Con, Leader-1, to search for it, and then turned his attention back to attacking the mighty Optimus Prime, sending the giant robot spiraling to the ground.

It didn't take Leader-1 long to locate the Mini-Con, and soon Megatron had it in the palm of his hand.

Megatron is the first to grab the Mini-Con.

The earthquake sends the ancient city tumbling down.

"Excellent, we've got what we came for. Retreat!" he ordered.

The Decepticons warped out of there just as the ground started to shake violently. The Transformers' battle had been too much. They had set off an earthquake. The ancient city was collapsing!

Carlos was upset to leave the hologram of the girl behind, but he, Alexis, and Rad each jumped into an Autobot in vehicle mode. As they made their escape the city was falling down around them!

No one spoke on the way home. This time, Megatron and his minions had won.

Watery tale
According to Plato, Atlantis was destroyed by the god Zeus and disappeared forever beneath the waves.

Lost kingdom
The ancient city of Babylon was said to have been destroyed in a great flood.

Volcano adventure

Everyone was pretty shaken up by Megatron's victory in the ruined undersea city. He had escaped with a Mini-Con named Sonar, one of the trio of Mini-Cons that made up the powerful Star Saber. Another one was Runway, the Mini-Con the kids had found at the South Pole.

With two of the three now located, Rad figured that there was a good chance the next Mini-Con signal they'd get would be the third piece. Something was worrying him. Did the Mini-Cons always have to be the cause of war?

crater

side vent

main vent

magma

Optimus Prime tells the kids about the history of Cybertron.

Optimus Prime gave the kids a quick history lesson about Cybertron. The Mini-Cons had such power that it was clear that Transformers would be fighting over them for a long time. And now the Mini-Cons were on Earth, the kids were involved, too.

Rad didn't have too much time to think about it all, because the alarm suddenly sounded.

"It's a new Mini-Con signal," said Hot Shot. "And it's coming from a volcanic island in the middle of the Pacific!"

Earth's interior
The inside of Earth is made up of the thin crust, the mantle, and the inner and outer central cores. The crust varies between 4 and 25 miles (6 and 40 kilometers) thick.

inner core

outer core

crust

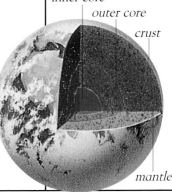

mantle

The Autobots in vehicle mode arrive on the island.

Fire god
The Romans believed that when a volcano erupted, it was because the God of Fire, Vulcan, was making thunderbolts inside the crater.

The kids ran to the warp gate and punched in the coordinates. It was vital that they got the Mini-Con before Megatron and his goons.

The Autobots and the kids warped in, materializing on the beach. The island was deserted, with the abandoned ruins of vacation homes on the slopes of the volcano. The wrecked remains of an old railway snaked around the mountain.

"Scans show it could erupt at any time," said Red Alert.

A column of thick, black smoke was already rising from the volcano's crater.

"We need to make this fast," agreed Optimus.

The Autobots set up their equipment and started local scans. Rad was still worried about anyone, even Optimus, using the Mini-Cons as weapons. After all, wasn't that why the Mini-Cons had fled Cybertron over four million years ago? It seemed to Rad that nothing much had changed.

As if to prove Rad's point, a grinning Megatron and his minions suddenly materialized. His cannon was pointing straight at the kids!

High point
The tallest active volcano on Earth is Ojos del Salado in South America. Its peak rises to over 22,000 feet (6,800 meters) high.

Megatron firing his massive cannon.

Sleeping giant
A volcano is said to be dormant when it has not erupted or shown any signs of activity for many years.

Ash cloud
Sometimes when a volcano erupts, it unleashes a cloud of hot, deadly ash as well as lava.

Megatron unleashed his tank cannon and fired wildly. Optimus blocked the shots.

"Take cover, kids!"

As they ran, they saw Hot Shot return the Deception's fire. A full-scale battle was breaking out.

While the big guys were locked in combat, Alexis wanted to go and find the Mini-Con. Rad took Laserbeak, his robotic scout, out of his pocket and watched him fly off.

The two sides were deadlocked on the battlefield until Starscream decided to combine with his own Mini-Con, named Swindle.

"Powerlink!" he shouted.

He got a fantastic boost in power and unleashed a frightening barrage of laser blasts down onto the hapless Autobots.

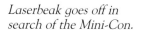

Laserbeak goes off in search of the Mini-Con.

34

"Very impressive. Now we can finish them off!" grinned the vile Megatron.

But it didn't quite work out that way. The kids' Mini-Cons, High Wire, Grindor, and Sureshock, leaped into the battle, forcing the Decepticons back again.

Higher up on the mountain, Laserbeak had located the Mini-Con, but as Optimus went to get it, the whole volcano started to shake!

High Wire, Grindor, and Sureshock come to the aid of the Autobots.

The evil Decepticons line up to battle the Autobots.

Volcano scientist
Volcanologists are scientists who study volcanoes—sometimes a dangerous job.

Smokescreen uses his utility crane to divert the path of the lava.

"The volcano is erupting!" shouted Alexis.

A huge flood of red-hot lava burst out of the crater. Laserbeak got away just in time. The lava crashed down the sides of the volcano carrying the Mini-Con with it.

The molten lava engulfed the volcano's upper slopes and was heading straight for the kids.

Smokescreen quickly transformed into vehicle mode and began to dig a deep trench to change the course of the lava's flow. Then the kids saw that the Mini-Con they were looking for was now floating along on top of the burning lava. Hot Shot tried to reach it, but the temperature was just too hot.

Swooping down from the sky,

Cyclonus, in helicopter mode, managed to snatch the Mini-Con out of the lava.

The Decepticons hadn't won yet though, because High Wire grabbed a laser cannon and, risking his own life, shot the Mini-Con right out of Cyclonus's hands.

Red Alert grabbed the Mini-Con, and the Decepticons warped out, defeated. The fight was over and the Autobots had won again.

Lava rock
When lava cools, it turns into solid rock. It is a type of rock called igneous rock.

Flying low, Cyclonus manages to grab the Mini-Con from the fiery lava.

Star Saber

After the battle of the volcanic island, the Autobots had two of the three Mini-Cons that made up the legendary Star Saber.

The other one was in the possession of Megatron, who had stolen it from right under the kids' noses in the undersea city.

They didn't know that, using intense radiation, Megatron had managed to awaken his Star Saber Mini-Con, called Sonar. Even worse, now it was awake, Sonar could sense the location of the other segments of the Star Saber.

The first the kids knew of this turn of events was a

Legendary weapon
The Star Saber is a legendary weapon from Cybertron's ancient past. It is very powerful and can slice through anything.

Megatron has possession of the Mini-Con, Sonar.

few days later when the alarms sounded in the Autobots' base.

"There's a warp gate opening inside our base!" said Optimus.

The kids watched on a monitor screen as the four Decepticons appeared in one of the base's corridors. Red Alert switched on the internal defense system—a little invention of his own in case of emergencies.

"They're heading straight for the command center. Open fire!" ordered Optimus Prime.

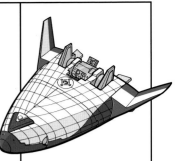

Sonar as an air-defense machine.

The kids watch in horror as the monitor screen shows that the Decepticons have materialized inside the Autobots' base.

Billy and Fred get more than they bargain for when they come to look around the base.

As the Decepticons advanced along the corridor, the automatic laser guns took aim and unleashed a barrage of laser fire!

Megatron and his creeps were pinned down until Alexis spotted something on the security monitor.

"Look, it's Billy and Fred!"

Carlos had been showing two of his school friends around the base, and they'd wandered off. Now they were trapped in the corridor behind the Decepticons.

"Stop firing!" said Optimus. "We might hit your friends."

"I'll teach the Decepticons to break into our base!" shouted Hot Shot, rushing out of the room to confront the evil robots. He was always the hot head.

The other Autobots quickly left to follow Hot Shot into battle, leaving Carlos, Alexis, and Rad in the control room.

Hot Shot found the Decepticons and leaped straight at Megatron. The Decepticon leader was much too strong for him, though, and easily threw him aside. Hot Shot was in serious trouble.

The Decepticons trap Billy and Fred in the corridor.

An angry Hot Shot rushes to attack Megatron.

Smoke signals
Native Americans sometimes used smoke to signal one another.

The Autobots slip away from the Decepticons as the corridor fills up with smoke.

Optimus Prime and the other two Autobots were quickly on the scene to help Hot Shot.

"You have something I want!" snarled Megatron.

But before Megatron could move, Smokescreen pressed a button on the wall, and the corridor was immediately filled with thick smoke. The Decepticons couldn't see a thing. Optimus grabbed Hot Shot, and the Autobots slipped away, hidden by the smoke.

"I've got a plan," Optimus declared. "Hot Shot, I want you to take the Mini-Cons and hide them somewhere in the base."

"Transform!" Hot Shot transformed into a sports car and went roaring off down a corridor.

The Decepticons caught sight of him and gave chase. As Hot Shot twisted and turned down the base's maze of corridors, the Decepticons had to split up.

Smokescreen crept up behind Demolishor and used the rope of his crane like a lasso. Demolishor was caught.

Elsewhere, Red Alert used a series of mirrors to get the better of Starscream. That was two Decepticons down and two to go!

Path puzzle
A maze is a series of winding paths and dead ends that makes it difficult to find a way out.

Runway
One of the three Mini-Cons that make up the Star Saber, Runway was recovered in Antarctica by the Autobots.

Sonar
One of the Star Saber pieces, Sonar was stolen by Megatron from the ancient undersea city.

While the heavy metal guys had been fighting, the kids had used the control room's scanners to track down Fred and Billy. Boy, were they glad to see their friends!

Unfortunately, Cyclonus interrupted their reunion, and they were soon playing a deadly game of hide-and-seek with the big freak. Rad tricked Cyclonus into following him into the room with the warp gate and used the controls to warp the great hunk of metal out of the base.

Optimus Prime and Hot Shot weren't doing so well. They'd tricked Megatron into stepping into an electric field, but he had escaped and

was now wildly blasting
everything around him.
A random blast hit Hot Shot,
and Megatron swiped the Mini-
Cons from his hand.

As each of the Star Saber Mini-
Cons sensed the presence of the
others, the trio combined into a
fantastic sword with a blade of pure
blue energy.

"The Star Saber is mine!"
shouted Megatron. "Now I alone
will rule the Universe."

Jetstorm
The final Mini-Con of the trio was rescued from an erupting volcanic island in the Pacific Ocean.

Megatron wields the powerful Star Saber.

Optimus is determined to stop Megatron from using the power of the Star Saber.

Old weapon
Another weapon of amazing powers was Excalibur, the legendary sword of King Arthur. It was given to him by the mysterious Lady of the Lake.

Optimus Prime clasped his hands together and sent out a wave of energy that knocked the Star Saber right out of Megatron's hand.

The weapon went spinning through the air and was caught by a rather surprised Hot Shot.

"Give that back to me!" boomed an enraged Megatron.

Hot Shot advanced on Megatron, but Megatron let rip with his massive tank cannon, blowing Hot Shot across the room.

It was up to the kids to save the day. Carlos, Alexis, and Rad arrived just in time.

"Focus on controlling the Star Saber!" Rad shouted to Hot Shot.

Megatron fired again, but this time Hot Shot concentrated all his thoughts on the Star Saber. He swung it at Megatron and sliced right through one of his shoulder plates.

"Aagh! Withdraw!" ordered Megatron. "Withdraw!"

In seconds they were gone, leaving the most powerful sword in the Universe in Hot Shot's hands. The quest for the Star Saber was over.

Hot Shot promises to use the Star Saber to fight for peace and justice in the battles ahead.

Glossary

Ambush
To wait in hiding and launch a surprise attack.

Ash
Hot embers that may fall during a volcanic eruption.

Bible
An ancient book containing the teachings of the Christian religion.

Chasm
A very deep crack in the earth.

Civil war
When two rival groups holding opposing political views fight for the right to rule their home country.

Convert
Change into.

Cosmos
The entire Universe.

Distress flair
A special device that fires a very bright light to alert others to your position.

Ferocious
Extremely fierce or cruel.

Flourish
To grow and prosper.

Hibernation
A very long winter sleep in which the sleeper saves energy.

Hologram
A special three-dimensional image that looks real.

Humanoid
Having the shape of a human being—a head and body, two arms, and two legs.

Illuminate
To shine light on.

Laser
A very powerful beam of light.

Lasso
A rope with one end in a circle so that it can be used to trap something or someone.

Lava
Red-hot molten rock that flows from a volcano during an eruption.

Loyal
Remaining true and faithful to your friends or your ideals.

Magma
Molten rock deep within the ground.

Materialize
To suddenly appear as if out of nowhere.

Medic
A doctor or nurse.

Meek
Quiet and gentle.

Minion
A slave or servant.

Monitor
A screen showing pictures, used to watch closely other people, things, or places.

Myth
A story handed down from long ago.

North Pole
Another name for the Arctic, an area of frozen water floating on the sea at the most northern point of the world.

Rotor
The part of a machine that goes around, like the blades of a helicopter.

Segment
Part of something.

South Pole
Another name for Antarctica, a continent of land located at the southernmost point of the world.

Transform
To change into something else.

Volcanologists
Scientists who watch and record the activity of volcanoes.

Wield
To control the action of something.

Index

Alexis 12, 13, 14, 16, 22, 26, 29, 34, 36, 40, 41, 46
Amundsen, Roald 14
angler fish 22
Antarctic cod 19
Antarctica 14, 15, 21, 44
Arctic 21
army helicopter 9
Atlantic Ocean 22
Atlantis 23, 24, 26, 27, 28, 29
Autobots 6, 7, 8, 9, 10, 11, 13, 14, 15, 19, 22, 24, 28, 29, 32, 33, 34, 35, 37, 38, 39, 41, 42, 44

Babylon 28
bathyspheres 22
Bible 28
blizzards 16

Carlos 12, 13, 14, 16, 18, 19, 21, 22, 23, 27, 29, 40, 41, 46
cars 4, 5, 8, 42
Cybertron 4, 6, 7, 9, 10, 11, 12, 13, 31, 33, 38
Cyclonus 9, 20, 37, 44

Decepticons 6, 7, 9, 10, 11, 13, 14, 17, 19, 20, 24, 27, 34, 35, 37, 39, 40, 41, 42, 43
Demolishor 9, 43

Earth 5, 12, 13, 14, 30, 31, 33
emergency rescue vehicle 8
Excalibur 46

eye surgery 40

Grindor 10, 12, 35
gulper eel 23

helicopters 16, 21
High Wire 10, 12, 35, 37
holograms 25, 26, 27, 29
Hot Shot 8, 14, 16, 17, 18, 19, 20, 22, 23, 24, 31, 34, 40, 41, 42, 43, 44, 45, 46, 47

icebergs 19
igneous rock 37

jet fighters 4, 5, 9
Jetstorm 45
Jolt 16, 18, 21

kids 12–13, 22, 27, 31, 32, 33, 35, 36, 38, 39
King Arthur 46

Laserbeak 34, 35, 36
lasers 25, 40
lava 30, 34, 36, 37
Leader-1 28

magma 30
mazes 43
Megatron 6, 7, 9, 15, 19, 24, 25, 28, 29, 30, 32, 33, 34, 35, 38, 40, 41, 42, 44, 45, 46, 47
Mini-Cons 10–11, 12, 13, 14, 15, 16, 18, 21, 22, 24, 25, 26, 27, 28, 30, 31, 32, 33, 34, 35, 36, 37, 38, 42, 45

Noah's Ark 28
North Pole 21

Ojos del Salado 33
Optimus Prime 6, 8, 14, 21, 22, 24, 25, 28, 31, 33, 34, 35, 39, 40, 42, 44, 46, 47

Pacific Ocean 31, 45
penguins 17
Perceptor 11
Plato 24, 29
Poseidon 28

Rad 12, 13, 14, 21, 22, 27, 29, 30, 31, 33, 34, 41, 44, 46
Red Alert 8, 14, 16, 20, 22, 32, 37, 39, 43
Runway 30, 44

smoke signals 42
Smokescreen 8, 36, 42, 43
Sonar 30, 38, 44
South Pole 14, 30
Star Saber 26, 30, 38, 44, 45, 46, 47
Starscream 9, 17, 19, 21, 34, 43
Sureshock 10, 13, 35
Swindle 34

tanks 4, 5, 7
Trieste 22

utility crane 36

volcanoes 30, 32, 34, 35, 36
volcanologists 36
Vulcan 32